Stained Glass
Table Runners ~ The Exquisite Table
by Brenda Henning

Credits

Written and illustrated by Brenda Henning
Printed in the United States of America

Special thanks to:
Treeforms Amish Furniture
4831 Old Seward Hwy, Anchorage, AK
for allowing their beautiful furniture to be the backdrop in my photographs.

ISBN 0-9773627-2-8

Stained Glass
Table Runners
~ The Exquisite Table
Bear Paw Productions
PO Box 230589
Anchorage, AK 99523-0589
(907) 349-7873

Copyright 2006 by Brenda Henning

No part of this book may be reproduced in any form without the written permission of the author. The written instructions, photographs, designs, and patterns are intended for the personal use of the retail purchaser and are under federal copyright laws. They are not to be reproduced by any electronic, mechanical or other means for commercial use. The information in this book is presented in good faith; no warranty is given.

Table of Contents

Project Supply Lists	2
Stained Glass Appliqué	
Fabric Selection and Preparation	3
Foundation Preparation	3
Freezer Paper Templates	4
Fabric Application	4
Centerfold - Stained Glass Patterns	
Bias Tape	5
Bias Tape Application	5
Bias Tape Numbering System	5
Layering the Project	7
Stitching Bias Tape in Place	7
Binding	8

Catalog

Current books and patterns can be viewed at:
www.bearpawproductions.com

Clover Quick Bias® also available from Bear Paw Productions in black, gold, silver, copper and black lamé.

Classroom Use

Use of the projects contained in this book is encouraged as a base for classroom instruction, provided each student is required to purchase a copy of the book.

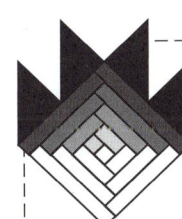

Bear Paw Productions
PO Box 230589 • Anchorage, AK 99523-0589
Phone (907) 349-7873 • Fax (907) 349-7875
www.bearpawproductions.com

Project Supply Lists

Forget-Me-Not Table Runner
16" x 44"
Fabric Requirements

Bias Tape - 11 yards - 1 reel

Background	fat quarter
Fabrics 1, 2, 3 and 4	fat quarter of each
Pink Squares - 8 squares 2 ½"	1/8 yard
Forget Me Not Fabric	
Yellow Center	3 ½" x 10 ½"
Blue Flowers	3 squares 8"
Green Leaves	3" x 21"
Backing and Batting	20" x 48"
Binding	¼ yard
Woven Fusible Interfacing	1 1/3 yards

Sunflowers Table Runner
16" x 41 ½"
Fabric Requirements

Bias Tape - 15 yards - 2 reels

Background	fat quarter
Border	fat quarter
Sunflower Fabrics	
Brown Center	8 ½" x 17"
Gold Petals	4 pieces 11" x 10"
Green Leaves	11" square
Backing and Batting	20" x 45"
Binding	¼ yard
Woven Fusible Interfacing	1 ¼ yards

Wild Roses Table Runner
16" x 45"
Fabric Requirements

Bias Tape - 11 yards - 1 reel

Background	½ yard
Fabric 1	4 ½" square
Fabric 2	1/8 yard
Fabrics 3 and 4	¼ yard
Fabric 5	1/8 yard
Rose Fabrics	
Yellow Center	2" x 4" piece
Pink Petals	5 pieces 4" x 8"
Green Leaves	8" x 16" piece
Backing	20" x 49"
Binding	1/4 yard
Woven Fusible Interfacing	1 1/3 yards

NOEL Table Runner
13 ½" x 40 ½"
Fabric Requirements

Bias Tape - 16 ½ yards - 2 reels

Background	½ yard
Bars and Swags	fat quarter
Letters, Posts and Binding	½ yard
Backing	18" x 45"
Quilt Batting	18" x 45"
Woven Fusible Interfacing	1 ¼ yards

Other basic supplies needed for Quilt As You Go Stained Glass:

Roxanne's Glue-Baste-It!®   freezer paper   pins
#60/8 sewing machine needles   sewing awl   cotton batting   safety pins
Clear or Smoke Invisible Poly Thread or other fine gauge thread in a color to match the bias tape

Quilt As You Go Stained Glass

Fabric Selection & Preparation

When selecting fabric for stained glass quilts I look for tone-on-tone prints to use in the design areas. Solid fabrics have been used by many, but I believe that mottled prints give the illusion of actual stained glass windows. Batik fabrics give the wonderful fluid appearance that I search for when designing the projects.

The fabrics used in these quilts are current as this book goes to print. Unfortunately, fabrics are forever being discontinued and new ones introduced. When searching for the perfect fabric for use in your quilt, please contact your local quilting shop; they are your best source for current fabrics.

Pre-wash all fabrics to be used in this project! This removes the sizing that may prevent the fusible bias tape from adhering properly. Spray starch and other fabric finishes should be avoided as they may also reduce the effectiveness of the fusible.

Foundation Selection & Preparation

Selection of the correct foundation is an important part of a successful project. I have chosen woven fusible interfacing for all of the projects found in this book.

The fusible interfacing that I use is a 100% cotton woven interfacing. (Non-woven products may not adhere well to your cotton fabrics. Knit tricot interfacing may shrink if steam or excess heat is applied!) The resulting finished product has the added firmness of the fusible while remaining soft and flexible. All areas of the interfacing will be covered with colored fabrics to create the design. The background fabric will be applied to the foundation as will the design elements.

Cut the fusible interfacing 2 - 3" larger than the full size pattern. This measurement can be found in the supply list of each pattern.

I highly recommend that you pre-wash the interfacing. This will prevent shrinkage of the interfacing as you apply the design fabrics with a steam iron. Hand wash the woven interfacing by carefully folding the interfacing. Soak in a basin of hot water (hot to the touch) for 30 minutes. Drain and squeeze out excess water, hang dry. This pre-shrinks the cotton fabric without damaging the fusible qualities of the interfacing. A few "beads" of fusible may brush off, but this is not a problem.

If you would rather not pre-wash the interfacing, take the time to do a shrinkage test. Cut a 4" square of interfacing and fuse it to a piece of cotton fabric using a hot steam iron. If the interfacing no longer measures 4" after it is fused, you should consider pre-washing it. If it shrinks and distorts with application of heat and steam, do not use it.

Center the fusible interfacing - with the fusible side up - over the pattern, and tape or pin in place to eliminate shifting. Trace the entire design onto the foundation using a Sharpie permanent marker. Use a ruler whenever possible to ensure straight lines. Do not transfer any numbers, boxes, or circles to the fusible interfacing. These markings may show through your design fabrics.

Freezer Paper Templates

Trace the pattern, **right side up**, onto the paper side of the freezer paper, using a #2 pencil or a Sharpie permanent marker.

You may label each piece of freezer paper to simplify assembly of the design. **Do not** label the foundation fabric, as these numbers may shadow through the design fabrics.

Cut the freezer paper exactly on the drawn lines with paper scissors. Do not add seam allowances.

Adjacent pieces that are of the same fabric may be cut as one unit. Pay close attention to directional fabrics. The resulting placement of a directional print may be undesirable.

Press the shiny side of the freezer paper to the **right side** of the selected design fabrics using a warm iron.

Fabric grain lines are not important. Place freezer paper template in such a way as to make the best use of the fabric design.

Cut the fabric slightly larger than the adhered freezer paper - 1/16" extra will allow the fabric raw edges to overlap a little when applying the pieces to the selected foundation. Use no more than a 1/16" allowance!

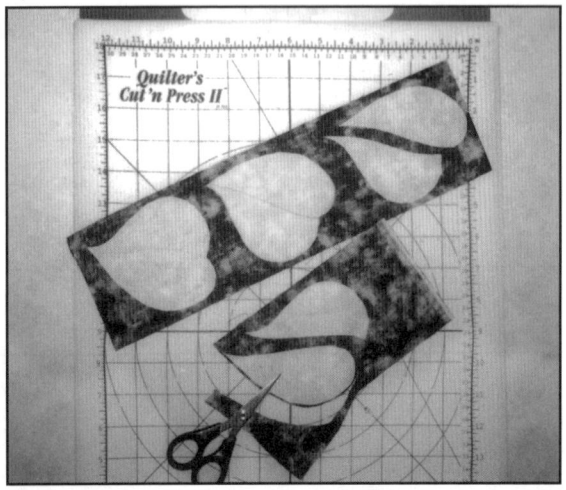

Remove the freezer paper from the cut fabric section. The freezer paper pieces may be saved and reused if you wish to make another project of the same design. Labeling the paper pieces is helpful.

Fabric Application

Place the interfacing foundation, fusible side up, on your pressing surface.

Position the design fabrics on the fusible interfacing foundation. Be sure that the applique' pieces are touching or overlapping a bit. Do not leave any gaps.

Place a pressing paper over the applique' pieces that have been positioned on the interfacing foundation. This will protect the surface of your iron from exposure to fusible web.

Press applique' pieces in place. Let the pressing paper cool completely and remove.

Continue fusing applique' pieces until the entire surface of the interfacing is covered.

Some design elements will be applied to the surface of the fused table runner. Retrace any placement lines that have been hidden by the "background" fabrics. Place dots of basting glue on the background fabric along the outline of the piece to be placed. Glue basting is diagramed below using **Roxanne's Glue-Baste-It!**

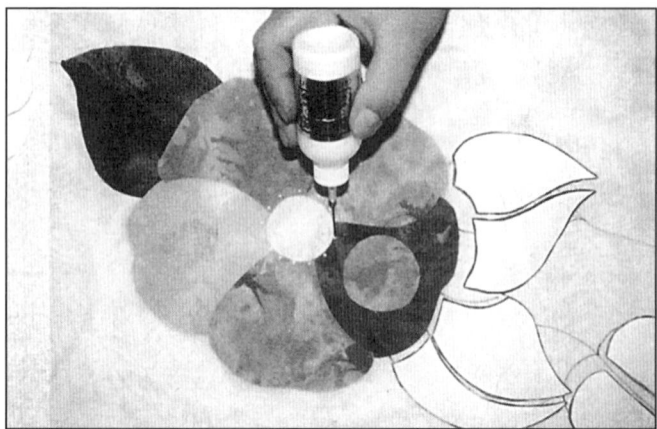

Carefully position the fabric piece on the background fabric. All dots of glue should be covered by the applied fabric. Allow the glue to dry.

After glue-basting all fabric pieces to the background, use a pencil to retrace any lines covered by the fabric appliqué pieces that have been cut as one unit - such as lines between the leaf halves.

NOTE If you anticipate the need to wash the completed stained glass quilt, consider securing the edges of the applique' pieces by overcasting with a machine zig-zag stitch before applying the bias tape.

Bias Tape

Clover Quick Bias is the bias tape used on the table runners in this book.

Clover Quick Bias is packaged 11 yards per spool.

NOTE: When using the **metallic** fusible bias tape, lower the temperature of your iron. This will lessen the possibility of damage to the bias tape caused by excess heat.

Homemade Bias Tape

You are not limited to commercial bias tape. The ability to create bias tape specific for your project opens up a world of possibilities. Print fabrics can be used, introducing texture and interest to the bias tape. Homemade bias tape is very economical. It is a terrific alternative if commercially prepared bias tape is not readily available in your area. Bias tape can be made entirely by hand without the use of any special tools.

Step 1 Cut bias strips 7/8" wide. One half yard of fabric will yield about 29 yards of 1/4" wide bias tape. Join the strips together using 1/8" diagonal seam allowances. Press open to reduce bulk.

Step 2 Fold one end of the bias strip into thirds and press (right side out). Fold and press 12" of the bias tape.

Step 3 Make a channel using two straight pins for the bias strip to travel through as diagramed below. A scant 1/4" channel is desirable.

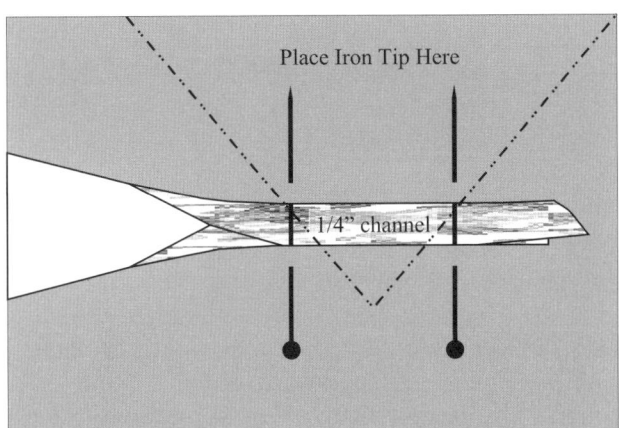

Step 4 Gently guide the strip through the channel, assisting the folding process as necessary. Once started, the strip should continue folding with only a little guidance. Position a warm iron over the folded strip to press it as the folds are formed.

Bias Tape Application

The purpose of the bias tape is to cover the raw edges of all fabric pieces and to simulate stained glass leading.

Bias tape will cover all raw edges of the applique'. The bias tape is centered directly over the junction of the applique' raw edges, over a single raw edge, or over the drawn leading line.

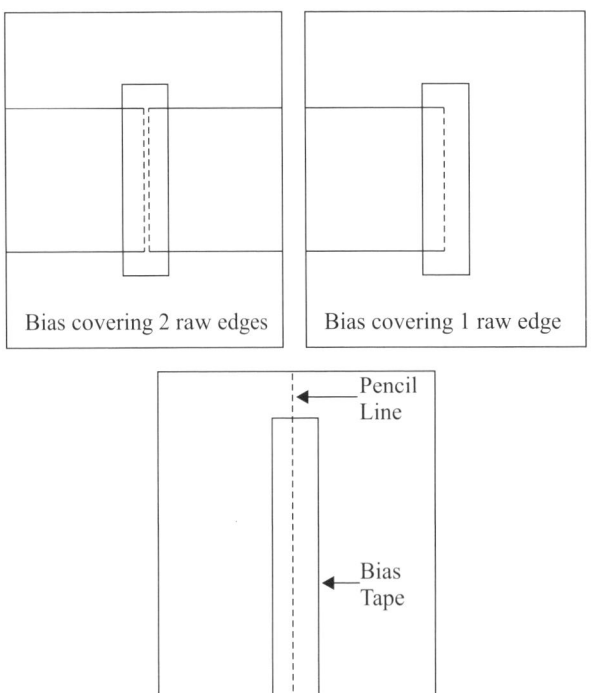

All bias tape ends must be covered!! Be sure to plan ahead.

The Bias Tape Numbering System

has been established to help you place bias tape in sequential order. This is not to imply that all pieces of bias tape will have a unique number in the sequence. Rather, there will be multiple pieces marked #1, multiple pieces marked #2, etc.

Lead all lines marked #1 first. Bias tape lengths marked #1 do not cover the raw end of any other piece of bias tape! All #1 pieces can be fused without disturbing the order of any other pieces. After placing all pieces marked #1, place all #2 pieces, which will cover raw ends of #1 pieces, and so on...

The only place that a raw edge - bias tape or fabric - is allowed, is at the very outer edge of the quilt. This will be encased in the quilt binding!

Mitered Corners - Miter the bias tape at each point. Press the fusible bias tape into place up to the point. Insert a pin into the edge of the bias tape where the point of the miter will be positioned. Pull the bias tape against this pin as you fold under the excess fabric, causing the mitered angle to form. In the case of a very sharp point, the fold may lay along the outer edge of the bias tape as shown below-right.

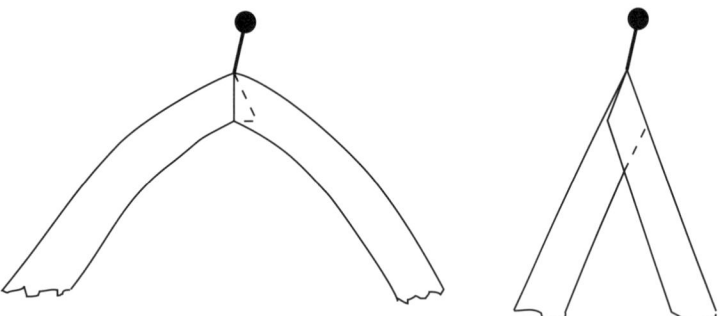

Boxed Intersections - The pattern may include bias tape intersections that are diagramed enclosed by a small box. The box indicates that the first piece of bias tape applied will need to be released from the design and another piece of bias tape inserted. Occasionally this cannot be avoided. Heat may be applied to the bias tape to make it easier to lift.

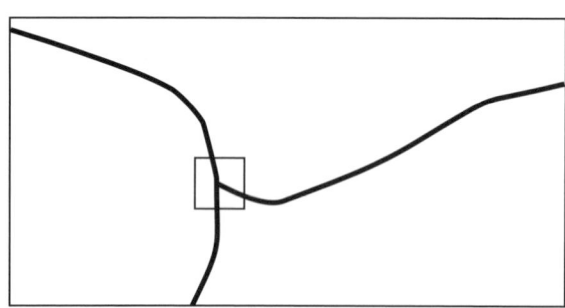

Circled Bias Tape Ends ~ Occasionally it is necessary for the bias tape to dead end in the center of a design without the benefit of being crossed by another piece of bias tape. At these points it is necessary to fold the raw end of the bias tape under itself to create a finished edge. Trim the bias tape 1/4" beyond the end of the drawn line and fold it under itself. The bias tape is very light weight and will fold nicely into place.

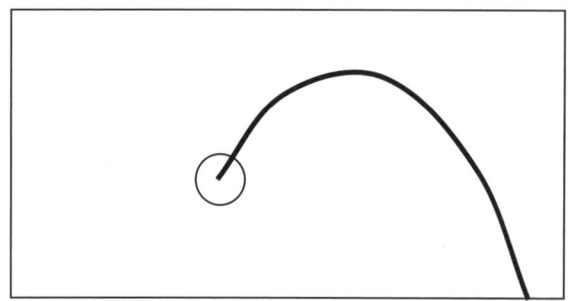

If you find that you have accidentally applied a piece of bias tape before its time, carefully pull the bias tape away from the applique' to release just enough space to insert the next bias tape end. You may use a pin to lift the prematurely-placed bias tape from the design.

Trim the end of the bias tape along the leading line that is intersected. This will allow the raw end of the bias tape to be covered (overlapped 1/8") by the next piece of bias tape. This may mean trimming the end of the bias tape at an unusual angle to accommodate the leading line.

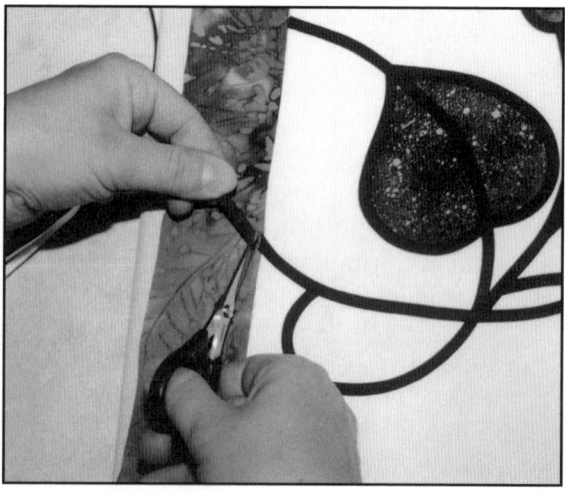

If you have positioned a piece of bias tape poorly, simply lift it from its place, reposition it, and press it in place with a warm iron!

It is my personal preference to apply all of the bias tape before the quilt is layered with batting and backing. During the construction of the sample quilts we found that the bias tape tended to release its grip on the large quilts. You may find it to your advantage to layer the project with batting and backing before the bias tape is applied. Pin baste thoroughly and apply the bias strips one at a time, stitching them in place as they are pressed onto the design.

Layering the Project

After all the bias tape has been pressed in place, layer the stained glass project with batting and backing.

Cotton batting works best. The cotton fibers of the batting grip the quilt top and backing. This helps to prevens shifting and puckering.

The backing and bobbin thread should match the color of the bias tape. If the bobbin thread pops to the surface of the quilt, it will not be noticeable. Less than perfect stitches will hide if the bobbin thread and quilt back match in color.

Baste the layers together using safety pins. Quilt basting spray may be used on the smaller projects. I have used Sulky® KK 2000 Temporary Spray Adhesive with good results. Fusible cotton batting is also very effective.

Stitching Bias Tape In Place

Insert a very fine needle into the sewing machine; size 60/8 works well. The holes left by the needle are very small, preventing the bobbin thread from popping to the surface. If you find you are breaking needles, change to a larger needle size, 70/10.

Thread the sewing machine needle with a fine gauge thread to match the color of the bias tape.

Bias Tape	Thread Choices
Black	Black Sew Bob (fine lingerie thread)
Gold	Clear poly filament thread
Silver	Clear poly filament thread

The bobbin thread may be cotton in a color to match the bias tape.

Use an open toe foot on your sewing machine, if you have one. It will be easier to see what you are doing. I find that my Bernina patchwork foot allows a clear view of my work area.

Stitch both sides of the bias tape in place using a straight stitch. Back stitch at both ends to secure to seam. Stitch at the very edge of the bias tape to avoid an unsightly pleat of bias tape that is not secured. Either side may be stitched first.

Clip threads close to the surface - front and back of the quilt.

Use a sewing awl to adjust and smooth bias tape if any puckering has occurred at tight curves.

If any bias tape should loosen as you are working, it can be secured again by gently pressing it back in place.

Binding

After all bias tape segments have been sewn, trim the completed quilt along the outer edge of the design.

Select a binding fabric in a color that will complement the design.

Cut strips 2" wide from binding fabric. Make the cut selvedge to selvedge. Stitch strips together on the diagonal as diagramed below. Trim seams to 1/4" and press open.

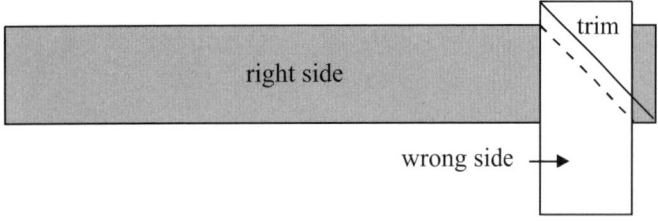

Press the strip in half lengthwise, wrong sides together.

Position the folded binding strip so that its lengthwise raw edges are even with the raw edge of the quilt top. Leave 8" free, and begin stitching the binding to the quilt a few inches beyond the center of one edge. Stitch with a 1/4" seam allowance; back tack to secure the seam.

Miter binding at the corners. Stop stitching 1/4" from the edge and back tack. Fold the binding strip up, away from the table runner; it will fold nicely at a 45° angle. Fold it again to bring the strip edge along the raw edge of the quilt top. This fold should be even with the top edge of the quilt. Begin stitching at the fold, stitch through all layers.

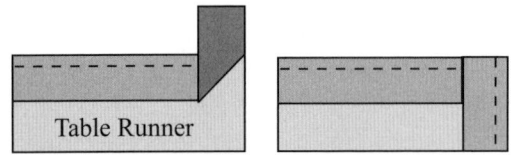

Continue sewing around the quilt in this manner until you are within 12" of the starting point.

To finish the binding, fold each strip back on itself so that the folds meet in the middle of the 12" gap. Finger press a crease at the folds. Trim the excess strip fabric 1" from both folds.

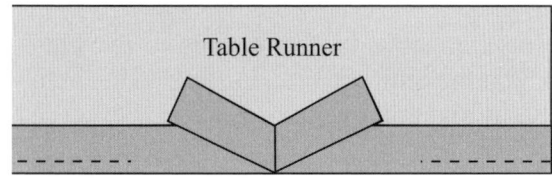

Open the folded strips and place the strips right sides together as diagramed below. Fold the table runner out of your way to allow the binding strips to be aligned properly. Stitch the strips together with a diagonal seam. Trim the seam allowance to 1/4" and press the seam open.

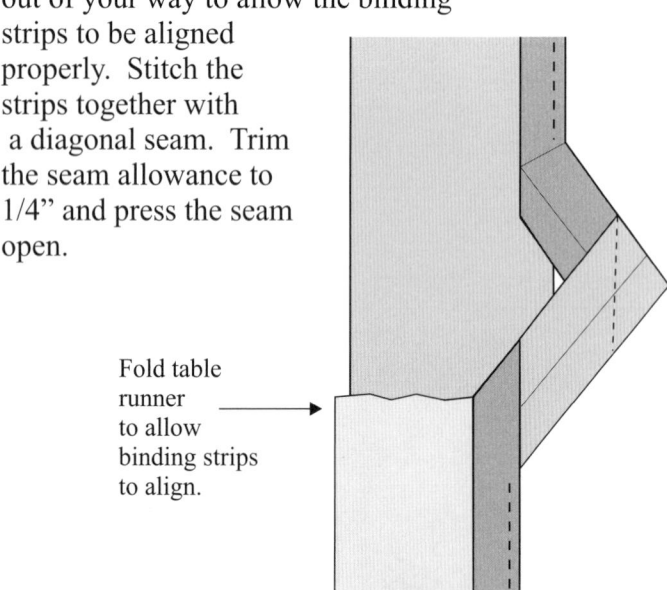

Fold the binding strip together again and finish stitching the binding strip to the edge of the project.

Hand stitch the folded edge of the binding to the back side of the table runner with a blind stitch. Use a thread that matches the binding. The fold of the binding should just cover the seamline.